IMAGES
of America

BEAVERTON

Since 2010, the Beaverton Historical Society has called the historic Thrifty Market building its home. The society meets monthly, often bringing in guest speakers to share their stories of days gone by and educate the public about the history of the area.

ON THE COVER: THRIFTY MARKET. The Thrifty Market building on Broadway Street was built in 1926 and was first known as the 20th Century Store. The name was later changed to the Thrifty Market. The owner, Otto Kiel, later opened Kiel's Grocery Store at another location. The Thrifty Market building housed Beaverton Blueprinting for many years and is now the home of the Beaverton Historical Society. Along with many buildings in its vicinity, it is listed in the National Register of Historic Places. (Courtesy of the Beaverton Historical Society.)

IMAGES
of America

BEAVERTON

Colleen Medlock

ARCADIA
PUBLISHING

Published by Arcadia Publishing
Charleston, South Carolina

Library of Congress Control Number: 2012934126

For all general information, please contact Arcadia Publishing:
Telephone 843-853-2070
Fax 843-853-0044
E-mail sales@arcadiapublishing.com
For customer service and orders:
Toll-Free 1-888-313-2665

Visit us on the Internet at www.arcadiapublishing.com

To my family.

CONTENTS

ACKNOWLEDGMENTS

I wish to thank the friendly and knowledgeable staff at the Beaverton Historical Society for collaborating with me on this project. Special thanks go to Michael Wong for his expertise with photographs and to Judy Donovan and Ann Koppy for helping me with research and for their willingness to answer my many questions. I also wish to thank Winn Herrschaft of the Washington County Historical Society for sharing her abundance of historical knowledge and for her encouragement. There are many people and organizations in the community who shared their photographs and memorabilia and I wish to thank them for their generosity and their willingness to participate in the making of this book. Unless otherwise noted, images appear courtesy of the Beaverton Historical Society and the City of Beaverton.

INTRODUCTION

The area of the Tualatin Valley that would become Beaverton was originally the home of a Native American tribe known as the Atfalati. They were hunters and gatherers and part of the larger Kalapuyan tribe. Although berries, camas bulbs, and nuts were the staples of their diet, the Atfalati usually traveled to Willamette Falls for the annual salmon run to supplement their diet with fish. The Atfalati population dwindled in the latter part of the 18th century due to a smallpox outbreak brought on by contact with European explorers and early American fur trappers, and again in the early 1830s after a malaria epidemic. They were no longer dominant in the area by the time settlers arrived in the 1840s—their numbers dropped to about 600 in 1842 and a mere 60 by mid-century. At one time, the Atfalati had about two dozen villages around the Tualatin Valley, including a summer camp they aptly called Chakeipi, meaning "Place of the Beaver."

Beaver were abundant throughout the Pacific Northwest and brought an influx of fur trappers seeking a part of the lucrative fur trade. The pelts were in high demand in the 18th and early-19th centuries, the industry spurred on by the popular men's fashion of the time—the beaver pelt top hat. By the time the pioneers began to arrive in the Tualatin Valley in the 1840s, the beaver had been hunted nearly to extinction, yet the evidence of the once profuse rodent population remained in the network of beaver dams dotting the landscape. The dams created lakes and swamps, earning the tribal village of Chakeipi the new moniker Beaverdam. The soil beneath the dammed water was nutrient-filled silt—a boon for the many farmers flowing into the region by way of the Oregon Trail.

In the mid-19th century, many Americans were stricken with Oregon Fever—the ardent desire to head west into the lands explored by Lewis and Clark beginning in 1804. The great majority of the emigrants were farmers and the lure of free land and the opportunity to start anew on the frontier made the Tualatin Valley a favored destination for many. The jumping-off point was Independence, Missouri, and the official end of the Oregon Trail was Oregon City. It was a journey that took at minimum six months, and was fraught with danger and sickness. The reward upon arrival: a full square mile of land—640 acres—for any man who arrived before 1850. All he had to do was get himself to the Oregon Territory and stake out his claim, either by using natural boundaries such as streams and rivers or by placing markers to delineate his property line.

In 1850, the federal government enacted the Donation Land Act in an effort to encourage more people to head west. This law required those already settled to reapply for their land and have a surveyor officially mark out the boundaries. The new law caused the land claims of many early settlers to be greatly reduced in size, as single men were now allowed to claim only 320 acres, and only if they had entered Oregon prior to 1850. Those who arrived after 1850 could claim 160 acres. Married men could claim 320 acres regardless of their arrival date, and their wives could claim an additional 320 acres. Consequently, marriageable women were in high demand on the frontier.

The settlers of the area now known as Beaverton had their work cut out for them when they arrived. Much of the fertile soil needed for farming lay beneath the shallow lakes created by the numerous beaver dams. Often farmers would plant crops on their higher land and were unable to use the underwater sections. Before long, however, there was a community effort to drain the beaver dams, with several of the early residents signing a charter and agreeing to drain their land into a series of ditches that subsequently flowed into larger creeks. Some farmers took matters into their own hands, like John Henry, who resorted to dynamiting the beaver dams on his land north of present-day Canyon Road, thereby releasing the water into Beaverton Creek.

It was a hardy and adventurous stock of people who left their homes and the comforts of civilization and ventured into what was then the unknown. Land claims were separated by long distances, causing feelings of isolation, and the long, dreary winters took a toll on their spirits, but the people who settled in Beaverton quickly set up the necessities of life and persevered. A log home was quickly erected, often replaced within a few years with a larger, more permanent home. Sawmills, gristmills, and shops sprang up, and before long, a young town was established complete with local government and postal and medical services. Within 50 years of the first land claim, Beaverton was incorporated, connected by rail to the larger city of Portland, and was a thriving, self-sufficient community.

One

EARLY RESIDENTS

A drive around Beaverton is like a drive through Oregon history: Denney Road, Hall Boulevard, Erickson Street, Watson Avenue, Allen Avenue, and Walker Road are just a few of the many streets named for the city's earliest residents. Many of these roads pass through the original land claims of pioneer families who crossed the plains by wagon in the 1840s and 1850s to claim their piece of real estate and set up life on the frontier.

The first land claim in the area went to Augustus Fanno, who arrived in 1846. The following spring, he claimed 640 acres along the creek that now bears his name. His was the 12th land claim filed at the Oregon land office, and the very first in the area that would become Washington County.

Thomas Denney was the next to claim land among the beaver dams. He had met Augustus Fanno in 1849, and Fanno encouraged him to settle on land adjacent to his. The recommended parcel of land was treed, free of underbrush, and contained a lake, which was just what Denney was looking for. He settled his claim in 1850 and the two families became joined the following year when Fanno married Denney's sister, Rebecca Jane Denney.

Kentucky native Lawrence Hall made the journey to Oregon at age 45, already the married father of several children. Hall and his family lived in a log cabin near what is now the intersection of Walker Road and Cedar Hills Boulevard, filing a land claim there in 1850.

Beaverton's Allen Boulevard is named for the scholarly and talented Orrin Sweet Allen. A veteran of the Civil War, he survived the Battle of Cold Harbor and the Battle of Crater before heading to Oregon in the 1870s with his wife, Frances Wade Allen, and their two children.

These are but a few of the pioneers who diligently farmed their land and withstood wet, lonely winters while molding the early community into a town. By the time Beaverton was incorporated in 1893, its population had grown to 400. As more families arrived in the annual wagon trains, land claims sprang up and families intermarried and grew. The McKays, the Betts, the Davies, the Walkers, the Tuckers—these early family names now live on in the names of streets, schools, and neighborhoods around the historic city of Beaverton.

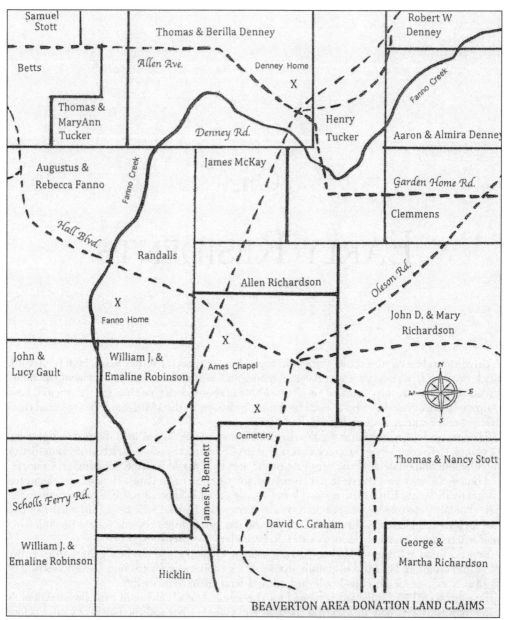

DONATION LAND CLAIM MAP. In 1850, Congress enacted the Donation Land Act with the intention of encouraging migration to the West, and it worked; the offer of free land caused many families to pack up and join the wagon trains heading to the Oregon Territory. Many families, including the Stotts, Denneys, and Tuckers, were from Indiana and naturally gravitated towards each other on the journey. When establishing their land claims, many of these families settled in the same vicinity. The marshy area that would become Beaverton began to fill in with these eager recipients of land grants, and the fledgling town began to materialize. (Map adapted from original, courtesy of Judy Donovan.)

AUGUSTUS FANNO FARMHOUSE. Augustus Fanno was born in Maine in 1804. In 1846, along with his wife, Martha Ferguson, and their young son, Eugene, he left Missouri for a six-month journey on the Oregon Trail. Sadly, Martha died in childbirth shortly after their arrival in Oregon City. In 1847, Fanno claimed 640 acres in the Tualatin Valley, where he developed a breed of onion that thrived in the wet climate of the northwest. By the 1890s, he had the distinction of being the largest distributor of onions in Oregon. Fanno married his neighbor, Rebecca Denney, in 1851, and together they had six children. When he built this two-story home, he made sure it was strong and sturdy so it could withstand the fierce winds he remembered from his Maine upbringing. Today, the historical house is owned by the Tualatin Hills Park and Recreation District.

THOMAS DENNEY. Fielding Denney was a veteran of the War of 1812 who raised his large family in Indiana. Thomas, his oldest son, went into the sawmill business near Concord. He met his cousin, Berilla King, around 1848, and by the spring of 1849, they were married, expecting their first child, and preparing to join the wagon trains heading west. Denney sold his gristmill but returned for his sawmill machinery, lest he need it out west. Once in Oregon, they stayed a year at a camp in Mills—now Milwaukie—where they met Augustus Fanno, who encouraged them to settle near his own creekside land claim. The Denneys settled near Fanno in 1850 and set up the first sawmill in the area. (Courtesy of Judy Donovan.)

BERILLA KING DENNEY. Berilla King Denney, born in 1822 in Indiana, was orphaned at an early age and lived with her brothers and sister on the farm left to them by their deceased parents. She married Thomas Denney in 1849 and, much to the dismay of her family, was determined to leave Indiana with him and head west. Berilla endured an arduous journey on the Oregon Trail as she was in the late stages of pregnancy as the wagon train crossed the Rocky Mountains and navigated the Snake River. In September 1849, she gave birth to her first child, Fielding John, near the John Day River in Eastern Oregon. The wagon train consented to a one-day layover for the birth of the baby and Berilla's recovery before pushing on for Oregon. (Courtesy of Judy Donovan.)

THE DENNEY HOUSE. Thomas Denney returned to Indiana to fetch his sawmill machinery, which he set up on Fanno Creek. He built a two-story plank house and moved his growing family out of the three-room log cabin they had been living in. The pioneer couple both lived into their 90s, with Thomas passing away in 1908, and Berilla in November 1912, as noted on her funeral receipt below. The house is long gone, although the addition seen at the left has been incorporated into the kitchen of the newer house on the same site. Today, Scholl's Ferry Road and Hall Boulevard run through the old land claim, and Denney descendants still live on the land. (Both, courtesy of Judy Donovan.)

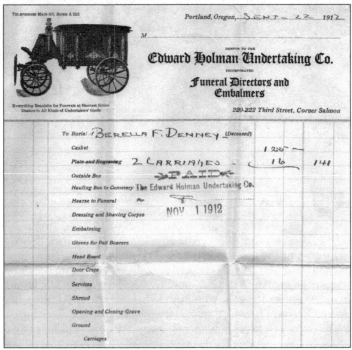

AARON VASCO DENNEY AND ALICE E. SMITH.
Thomas Denney's youngest son, Aaron, was born
in Oregon in 1861 and grew up on the land claim
Thomas and Berilla Denney had registered in
1850. He was 40 years old when he married Alice
E. Smith in 1901. They had two sons and built an
expansive home near the elder Denneys. Aaron
was a farmer and county fruit inspector as well
as an active board member for School District
No. 18. (Both, courtesy of Judy Donovan.)

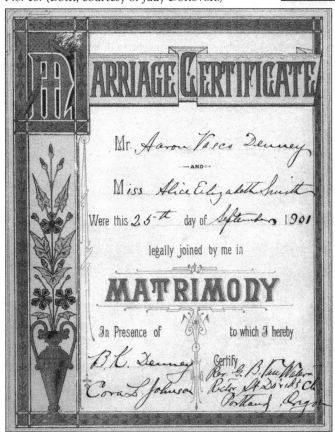

AARON AND ALICE DENNEY, EARLY 1900S. Aaron Vasco Denney and his wife, Alice, built this lavish home in 1902. It was located near present-day Scholls Ferry Boulevard and Allen Avenue. Alice was known for her musical talent on the piano and her hospitality, often cooking meals for all the farmhands during harvest time. She was very organized, keeping a journal in which she diligently noted the names of her many visitors as well as household tips and recipes. Her two sons, Kenneth and Rex, were just 13 and 11 when Alice passed away in 1917. Aaron continued to manage the farm until 1931, when he passed away at the age of 69. (Both, courtesy of Judy Donovan.)

THE PETERSON FAMILY, C. 1905. John and Matilda Peterson pose for a family photograph with their three daughters Anna (or Emma, according to the 1900 census), Beryl, and Margaret. Peterson was a farmer, and the family lived on Beaverdam Road, near present-day Center Street and Hall Boulevard.

WILLIAM O. AND EMMA HOCKEN. Beaverton's Hocken Avenue is named for William O. Hocken, who left England in 1870 to try his hand as an Oregon farmer. He owned land at Fourth Street and Watson Avenue, which he donated to the Methodist Church, and then built a one-room building for the congregation to meet in. He also served as mayor in 1913.

T. B. TUCKER
W. M. 1895

THOMAS TUCKER, 1895. The Tuckers were an Indiana family who relocated to Oregon in 1852 when the oldest son, Thomas, was 21 years old. Thomas helped his father, Henry Bellinger Thomas—for whom Beaverton's Tucker Avenue is named—establish a 320-acre land claim near the Denney family. He served as county commissioner for two terms and was an active member of the Beaverton Masonic Lodge, serving as a junior warden in 1891 and as master in 1895. (Courtesy of Beaverton Masonic Lodge No. 100.)

MARY AND WILLIAM TUCKER FAMILY, C. 1890. The younger Tucker son, William, was 19 years old when he crossed the plains in 1852. He claimed 120 acres near his brother, Thomas, and the two started a sawmill business. William fought in the Cayuse War in the 1850s, returning to marry Mary Landess, with whom he had 11 children. The Tucker family included, from left to right, (first row) Will, Mary, Carl, William, and Lottie; (second row) Elizabeth, Thomas B., Abraham Lincoln, Delilah, Ira, Adeline, and Eva. Son George Washington is not pictured.

ALONZO BROCKWAY CADY.
Alonzo Cady was born in 1823 in Moravia, New York. In 1850, he moved to Wisconsin with his wife, Eliza Gilbert, where he went into the shoe business. After fighting for the Union in the Civil War, he moved to Kansas and went into business with his son, Fred Willis Cady. A year after losing his wife in a tornado in 1885, he married a widow named Ann Martin. In 1892, at the age of 69, Alonzo relocated to Oregon at the urging of his daughter, Marian, who had left for Oregon a few years earlier. He quickly became a prominent member of the community, serving as Beaverton's first mayor in 1893, as leader of the town's fledging Masonic organization in 1894, and as county treasurer for four years. The Cady home (below) was at the corner of Angel and Seventh Streets. Alonzo Cady died in 1907 at the age of 83. (Both, courtesy of Beaverton Masonic Lodge No. 100.)

FRED WILLIS CADY. Alonzo Cady's youngest child, Fred Willis Cady, was born in 1861 in Wisconsin. As a young man in Kansas, he went into the boot and shoe business with his father, leaving in 1888 to go to business college in Portland. He returned to Kansas briefly in the early 1890s, where he married Mary Hills, known as Mame. His older sister, Marion, who had lived on the west coast since 1863, encouraged him to return, so Cady, along with his father, Alonzo, and his brother, Miles, made his way to Beaverton by way of Ellensburg, Washington, and McMinnville, Oregon, where he operated shoe businesses with his father. He became Beaverton's postmaster general in 1895 while he continued in general merchandising. In 1905, he opened the Cady-Anderson store on Broadway Street, where he sold everything from groceries to textiles, and operated the post office out of one end of the store.

FRED WILLIS AND MAME CADY, 1923.
Fred Willis Cady was a prominent
member of the community once he
settled in Beaverton. In addition to
running the successful Cady-Anderson
store and holding the position of
postmaster general for more than two
decades, Cady served as master of the
local Freemasons in 1909. He was also
the mayor of Beaverton from 1909 to
1910, and again from 1917 to 1919. The
photograph below of Fred and Mame
was taken in 1923, two years before Fred
died from injuries sustained in a car
accident. After his death, Mame took
in boarders to help make ends meet
while the country's economy floundered
towards the Depression. She passed
away in 1931. (Right, courtesy of the
Beaverton Masonic Lodge No. 100.)

F.W. CADY
W.M. 1909.

Geo.Wm STITT
W.M. 1892...1901

GEORGE STITT, C. 1900.
George W. Stitt was born in 1841 in New York, and came to Oregon in 1878 with his wife, Mary. They raised five children and grew onions on their farm (below) in Beaverton. Stitt was a very involved citizen, serving as the worshipful master of the Beaverton Masons in 1892 and again in 1900 and 1901. He was an active member of the Congregational Church and was known as a generous supporter of the church and his community. He died in 1924. (Both, courtesy of Beaverton Masonic Lodge No. 100.)

Dr. Francis Robinson. Francis Marion Robinson was born in Oregon in 1848 and raised on a farm in Hillsboro. He studied at Pacific University in Forest Grove and graduated from Salem's Willamette University in 1885. Robinson married Wisconsinite Lottie Danks in 1889 and together they raised three children in an ornate, Queen Anne–style home on Broadway Street. He set up his medical practice on Broadway as well, where he became known for making house calls in his horse and carriage any time of day, not only to Beaverton patients, but also to the towns of Progress and Garden Home. He had a pharmacy built next door for the convenience of his patients. Today, the house and pharmacy have been converted into the popular Beaverton Bakery. Dr. Robinson was also a city councilman, the first master of Beaverton's Freemasons, and mayor in 1903. (Courtesy of the Beaverton Masonic Lodge No. 100.)

J. N. FISHER
W.M. 1893, 1899, 1902

JOHN N. FISHER. The son of a German immigrant who bore the same name, John N. Fisher was born in Ohio in 1839, but was an orphan by the age of eight and practically raised himself. He spent three years fighting in the Civil War and was wounded twice at the Battle of Vicksburg. After the war, Fisher spent some time in New Jersey, Nebraska, and San Francisco before arriving in Portland around 1875. He was instrumental in founding the *Portland Daily Bee* newspaper and, later that year, settled in Beaverton and took up farming. He also ran a successful meat market and was an insurance agent. In 1877, at the age of 38, he married Della Allen, and they had seven children. Fisher was an active Mason, serving in the capacity of master three times in 1893, 1899, and 1902. (Courtesy of the Beaverton Masonic Lodge No. 100.)

EARL FISHER
W. M. 1905..

EARL FISHER. John N. Fisher's son, Earl, was born in Beaverton in 1879. Like his father, he was a member of the local Freemason organization, serving as master in 1905. He also served five separate terms as mayor, in 1906, 1907, 1908, 1933, and 1951, holding the distinction of being both the youngest mayor of Beaverton (age 26) and the oldest (age 80). Fisher was involved in writing and directing community plays, establishing the first volunteer fire brigade, organizing sports teams, and publishing the local newspaper *The Owl* in addition to serving as a state senator for two terms and teaching in the district for 26 years. He did not marry and had no progeny, but lived a long and productive life, passing away in 1961 at the age of 81. (Courtesy of the Beaverton Masonic Lodge No. 100.)

E.D. SUMMERS
W.M. 1904, 1911..

EDGAR D. SUMMERS. Edgar Summers was born in Illinois in 1860 and came to Oregon at the age of 30. A carpenter by trade, he was involved in the construction of many of Beaverton's earliest buildings. He was an active member of the Congregational Church and the local Masonic organization, serving in the capacity of master in 1904 and again in 1911. (Courtesy of the Beaverton Masonic Lodge No. 100.)

CLASSEN FAMILY. Dutch-born Lambert Classen and his German wife, Mary, settled in Beaverton in 1904. The 1910 census indicates that they originally spelled their name "Claussen." The family owned and operated 13 acres of hothouses off Canyon Road near present-day Murray Boulevard, growing lettuce and cucumbers to sell in Portland. The family photograph above shows three of the four Classen children: Gerhard, the oldest, and twins Arnold and Berdina—"Dena." The cucumber and lettuce hothouses are seen to the left of the Classen home below.

DENA CLASSEN. The Classen farm was conveniently located near the train tracks, although Beaverton was not a regular stop. Their daughter, Dena Classen, shown above in 1915, would wait by the tracks and flag down the conductor when the family had produce to send via rail to Portland's markets. On the left, Dena (far right) poses with friends Agnes (Kennedy) Luchs (left) and Emma Huber (middle).

DENA CLASSEN MAYFIELD AND DAUGHTERS. Dena Classen married Oklahoman Henry Mayfield and raised three daughters: Florence, Dottie, and Laurie. Always interested in law enforcement, Henry Mayfield became the city's first chief of police.

THE DEANS, C. 1920s. Lewis R. Dean was a prominent businessman in early Beaverton, operating a drugstore with his wife, Mary, on Farmington Road and later on Broadway Street. The family, shown here with their daughter, LaMerne, but without their son, Harold, moved into their five-bedroom house at Third and Main Streets in 1918. The house still stands and is currently the home of Beaverton Clinic of Chiropractic.

THE MERLO FAMILY. John and Annunziata Merlo emigrated from Genoa, Italy, with their large family of seven girls in 1910. Annunziata's parents had immigrated to the area a few years earlier and were successfully running an onion farm. Within a few years of their arrival, John and Annunziata had purchased the Commercial Hotel at Farmington Road and Watson Avenue and were running a boardinghouse and restaurant there. Posing for the family photograph above are, from left to right, (sitting) Eva, John, Dena, Annunziata, and Rose; (standing) Theresa, Leona, Louise, and Ada. Below, Eva and Rose relax with a boarder on the porch of the Commercial Hotel in 1917. Merlo Road, Merlo High School, and Merlo Station are all named for the Italian immigrant family.

THE ROSSI FAMILY, 1909. Augustus "Gus" Rossi was born in Italy in 1871 and came to the United States with his family as an infant. He married Beaverton native Hattie Wolf in 1894, with whom he raised four children. After 20 years of farming, he opened a saloon on Broadway Street, which nearly caused his membership in the local Freemason organization to be revoked. When it went to a vote, it was decided that Rossi could be a tavern owner and still be considered an upstanding citizen and a part of the fraternal organization. Rossi was also a member of the city council. This family photograph includes, from left to right, Frank, Hattie, Albert, Gus, Elva, and Raymond.

Augustus Rossi Emblem. Gus Rossi had his initials and this beaver emblem carved into the plaster of the building he was constructing when he passed away in 1926. These emblems can still be seen on the Rossi building at the corner of West and Broadway Streets. Below, one of the Rossi children takes a wagon ride with friends.

FRANK LIVERMORE, 1930. Frank Livermore operated a sawmill in Beaverton, moving it three times. Its first location, on Weir Road near Cooper Mountain, opened in 1896 and burned a year later. The second sawmill was on present-day 185th Avenue, southwest of Hart Road, and the third was at what is now 170th Avenue and Farmington Road. The Livermore home (below) was near the third sawmill. Livermore was also the commissioner of Washington County and the county judge for some time, as well as president of the Beaverton Bank until it closed in 1930.

THE WELTER FAMILY. The Welters were a German immigrant family who lived in Chicago and Indiana before settling in Beaverton in 1890. Near their home at Third and Lombard Streets, they built greenhouses and grew lettuce in the winter and cucumbers in the summer. Michael Welter loaded up his covered wagon once a week to take his produce to the Portland markets. When automobiles took over, the Welters became the proud owners of one of the first Buicks in town and were often spotted out on family drives with the top down.

MARY WELTER, 1918. Mary Welter poses near an "invalid car," or ambulance, during her nurse's training in 1918. Like many American towns, Beaverton was hit hard by the influenza epidemic of 1918, losing many residents to the illness. Beaverton schools were even closed for three months that fall.

WINFIELD E. PEGG AND LEWIS DEAN. Winfield E. Pegg (left, in bowler hat) and Lewis Dean (of Dean's Drugs) stand in front of Dean's home in the 1920s at Third and Main Streets. Pegg, the town mortician and one-time mayor, lived next door.

OTTO ERICKSON AND AUGUSTA ARONSSON. Otto Erickson was a Swedish immigrant who arrived in Portland in 1888. He was 19 years old at the time, and spent his first year learning English and taking courses in accounting. He spent some time as a miner in Telluride, Colorado, before returning to Portland to work for the Oregon Railroad and Navigation Company and marrying Augusta Aronsson in 1895. Born in 1872, she was also from Sweden and had been working as a domestic in The Dalles when Erickson met her on one of his steamboat stops along the Columbia River. They made their home in Ophir, a mountain town near Telluride, but traveled frequently between Colorado and Oregon. (Courtesy of Robert Lindstedt.)

OTTO ERICKSON AND FAMILY. The Ericksons had two daughters: Florence, born in 1897, and Edith, born two years later. When Augusta Erickson died in 1905, the young girls were sent to live with relatives in Portland. Sadly, Florence succumbed to typhoid fever in 1910 at the young age of 13. Erickson went to Mexico and mined in the Nogales region as a manager of the Yellow Mountain Gold Mining Company, until he was chased out by Pancho Villa. He remarried in 1911, and in 1912, returned to Oregon where he bought land in Beaverton along what is now Erickson Avenue. Known as a hot-tempered, foul-mouthed man but a savvy businessman, Erickson went into the automobile business, becoming the area's first Ford dealer, with shops in Forest Grove, Hillsboro, and Beaverton. He was an influential and outspoken resident whose foray into politics included three one-year terms as mayor, beginning in 1919. (Courtesy of Robert Lindstedt.)

G.C. CARR
W.M. 1930.

GUY CARR. Guy Crockett Carr's parents had divorced when he was very young, and his mother, Maybelle Carr, went to work in a hotel in Ophir, Colorado, where she met her second husband, Otto Erickson. Carr was raised by his father's family in Virginia until he was sent out on his own at the age of 15. He did not reunite with his mother until after serving in World War I and learning of her whereabouts through a friend in boot camp. Carr came to Beaverton in 1919 to meet his mother and decided to stay, going to work for his stepfather demonstrating and selling Fordson tractors. He married Mildred Anderson in 1926 and they had two daughters by 1932. Carr bought out Erickson's Beaverton Ford dealership in 1923 and continued selling cars until he retired in 1987. Carr Chevrolet on Canyon Road carries on his name. (Courtesy of the Beaverton Masonic Lodge No. 100.)

E. STIPE
W.M. 1920

ELMER STIPE. A man of many interests, including airplanes, automobiles, and law enforcement, Elmer Stipe opened a Chevrolet dealership called Stipe's Garage in 1916, later moving it to Broadway Street in 1921. His interest in all things aeronautical resulted in a uniquely designed airplane known as the "Stiper." Stipe was also hired as Beaverton's town marshal in 1917, for which he was paid $1.50 for each arrest. (Courtesy of the Beaverton Masonic Lodge No. 100.)

Two

BUSINESS AND COMMERCE

Since 1986, the downtown core of Beaverton has been listed in the National Register of Historic Places as the Beaverton Downtown Historic District. This designation gives business owners a tax break when rehabilitating or taking measures to preserve old buildings, helping to ensure that Beaverton's historic buildings last well into the future. Perhaps more importantly, the designation is an honor recognizing the historic value of the downtown area and its original business district.

Many of the buildings from the city's first few decades are still in use today, although they may have been remodeled or updated over the years. Dr. Robinson's grand house on Broadway Street, for instance, is part of the Beaverton Bakery, and the Bank of Beaverton at the corner of Farmington Road and Watson Street is currently an Arthur Murray dance studio. The Cady Building still stands regally at the corner of Watson and Farmington and is home to several small businesses, just as it was almost 100 years ago when Dr. Hetu practiced dentistry upstairs and Lewis Dean operated a pharmacy on the ground floor.

Some early Beaverton businesses, although not necessarily in their original locations, continue to thrive today. Rose Merlo's venture into the horseradish business in the 1920s has evolved into the successful Beaverton Foods Company and has expanded production to include mustards under the brand names Beaver and Inglehoffer. The award-winning condiment company is still run by Rose's progeny and is still headquartered locally. Likewise, while Swedish immigrant Otto Erickson's Ford dealerships are no longer, the Beaverton location his stepson Guy Carr bought from him continues to operate, after several relocations, as Carr Chevrolet on Southwest Canyon Road.

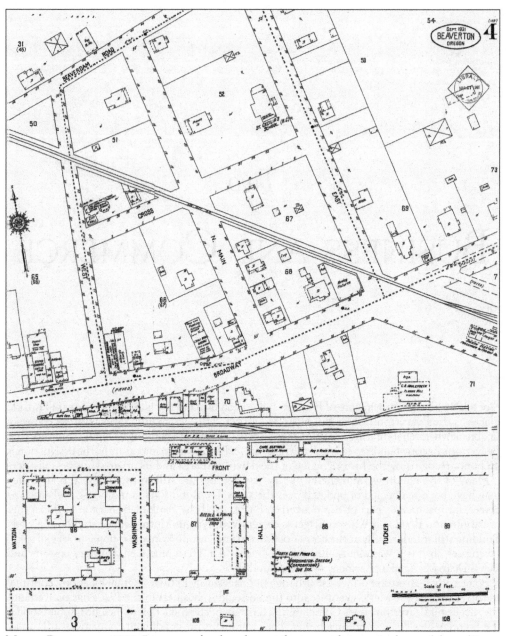

MAP OF BEAVERTON, 1921. Beaverton developed as a rail town, with its main thoroughfare of Front Street—later renamed Farmington Road—paralleling the tracks and the shops of Broadway Street springing up within walking distance of the depot. (Sanborn map courtesy of the Washington County Historical Society.)

EDWARD SQUIRES'S BLACKSMITH AND CARRIAGE SHOP, 1892. The earliest businesses in Beaverton sprang up along the dirt thoroughfare known as Broadway Street. Every pioneer town needed a blacksmith, and Edward Squires filled the need for Beaverton's early residents. His carriage and blacksmith shop is pictured above on the left, with his house on the right. His wife, Frances, stands at the gate. Below is a handwritten receipt for services rendered. (Below, courtesy of Judy Donovan.)

SOMETHING NEW.

SQUIRES' "DEXTER KING"

Buggies, Hacks and Carts.

PATENTED JUNE 29, 1886.

This Gear is especially adapted for a Brake.

In its simplicity, durability, style of finish, ease of motion, and elegance of appearance, has no equal, and is better adapted to rough roads than any other buggy made. The axles, being attached to the springs, can easily give when the wheels strike uneven ground, and therefore lessens the shock to horse and driver; the wheels thus giving a little, have their durability increased. They spring down nearer square than any other gear or form of side spring buggy.

I am now making them in four styles—Side Springs, End Springs, Three Springs, and Four Springs. I keep on hand, and make to order at Lowest Prices, my

PATENT CARRIAGES.

My Patent Carriages have been in use for about three years and are giving good satisfaction.

Please call and see my Seventy-five Dollar Buggies and my Hacks with two Seats and Pole, all trimmed in good style, for One Hundred and Twenty Dollars, and Carts from Thirty-five Dollars to Fifty, with my Patent Improvement on them. All work warranted. My motto is—

SMALL PROFITS AND QUICK SALES.

I also deal in all kinds of AGRICULTURAL IMPLEMENTS at Lowest Prices. My Buggy Gears are made entirely of Steel and Iron, which makes them more lasting than any other gear made, for all climates, *and will not cost to keep them in repair one-half what any other make does where wood and iron are combined.* We furnish Gears for Thirty Dollars, less 10 per cent. for Cash, shipped on cars at Beaverton.

TESTIMONIALS.

Office of Wheeler & Wilson Mfg. Co.,
88 Morrison St.,
PORTLAND, OR., Sept. 12, 1887.
MR. E. SQUIRES, Beaverton, Or.—*Dear Sir:* We have used one of your "Dexter King" wagons for nearly three years, and must say it has cost us less for repairs than any other wagon we have had in the business—and we take great pleasure in recommending it and acknowledging that it has given perfect satisfaction.
Yours truly,
E. HIGHAM,
Manager.

BREAVERTON, OR., July 31, 1887.
To all whom it may concern—
I hereby certify that I have used, to a limited extent, several buggies manufactured by Edward Squires of Beaverton, Oregon, and have found them satisfactory in every respect—*light draft,* and substantial.
I think the style so well adapted to this country that I have ordered one of first-class material and build for my own use.
F. M. ROBINSON, M.D.

Office of Drs. Nichols,
Physicians and Surgeons,
PORTLAND, OR., July 29, 1887.
E. SQUIRES—*Dear Sir:* In reply to your letter, I would say that the buggy is very satisfactory—rides easy, no rattling, carries level, in fact, everything O K.
Yours,
C. L. NICHOLS.

Office of Raymond Bros.,
Dealers in General Merchandise,
GASTON, OR., Aug. 26, 1887.
MR. SQUIRES—*Dear Sir:* We are very much pleased with the buggy you sold us. It rides splendid. Everyone who sees it seems pleased with it.
Yours truly,
C. A. RAYMOND.

GASTON, OR., Aug. 25, 1887.
E. SQUIRES—*Dear Sir:* I am well pleased with my buggy, and if I was going to buy forty, would buy your make.
Yours truly,
A. L. MC. LEOD.

Address all orders to   EDWARD SQUIRES.

SQUIRES WAGON ADVERTISEMENT. Edward Squires patented a design for horse-drawn wagons that, with axles attached to springs, provided a smoother ride than many wagons of the day. His motto was "small profits and quick sales," earning him the respect of many prominent Beaverton businessmen who spoke highly of him and provided positive testimonials in the local newspaper. (Courtesy of Judy Donovan.)

Gus Rossi's Saloon. Gus Rossi opened the saloon at Broadway and West Streets in 1900 after becoming frustrated with farming, having seen too many crops succumb to frost in his 20 years in the fields. He called his saloon the 1900 Saloon in reference to the year it opened, and it quickly became a popular watering hole in town. Rossi closed the saloon in 1915 and returned to farming, although he was constructing a new saloon in 1926 when he died of a heart attack. His family finished the construction of the new saloon and kept it in the family.

HOTEL BEAVERTON.
The Hotel Beaverton
welcomed travelers
and offered food and
lodging in a convenient
location. The two-story
building on Farmington
Road, located just across
from the train depot,
changed names several
times over its lifetime.
It was called the Hotel
Beaverton at first, then
the Commercial Hotel
when the Merlo family
purchased it and operated
it as a boardinghouse.
The building
underwent an extensive
renovation, gaining
a new covered porch
and peaked roofline.

BROADWAY STREET SHOPS, EARLY 1900S. The Cady-Anderson Store, opened in 1905 by Fred Willis Cady, was known as "The Satisfaction Store." It was well stocked with the staples local townspeople needed: beans, rice, baking powder, salt, flour, lard, yeast, and the like. Cady also sold fruits and vegetables purchased from area farmers and would often make deliveries in his horse-pulled wagon.

THE MORSE BUILDING, 1911. The two-story Morse Building at West and Broadway Streets was a gathering place for the community featuring shops and a pool hall on the ground floor and a ballroom with a balcony upstairs. Portlanders often rode the train out to Beaverton to attend dances at Morse Hall, and lessons were often offered as well.

THE WHITE HOUSE SALOON, 1916. In 1914, voters approved an amendment to the Oregon constitution banning the sale and advertisement of alcohol. When this photograph of the White House Saloon on Broadway Street was taken in 1916, the law had recently gone into effect, although the advertisement for Heidelberg Beer remains defiantly on the front of the saloon. To the left is the Fisher Building in its early stages of construction and on the far left is the town bandstand, which Fisher also helped build.

BEAVERTON POST OFFICE. Andrew M. Kennedy, W.B. Emmons, Victor Emmons, and Bill Boyd have their hands full as they set out to deliver the mail. Beaverton's first post office was a log building constructed by George Betts on the corner of Farmington Road and Angel Street. The structure had formerly been used as a store. Betts became the town's first postmaster general, and is the namesake for Betts Avenue, where the current Beaverton post office is located. Below, Bill Boyd delivers mail via horse and buggy in 1910.

ANDREW KENNEDY, 1910s. Andrew M. Kennedy came to Beaverton in 1877 to try his hand at farming and ended up becoming one of the city's first mail carriers, from around 1910 to 1920. At first, he delivered the mail in a horse and buggy before upgrading to an automobile. He was a fan of the Brush automobile (below), which was billed as "Everyman's Car" for its reliability and simplicity.

BROADWAY STREET LOOKING WEST, C. 1910. Beaverton's early business district contained a mix of commercial and residential buildings. As a rail town, pedestrian-oriented businesses sprang up within a short distance of the railroad tracks, and wide streets accommodated the transportation of the time—the horse and carriage. At the time this photograph of Broadway Street was taken, Morse Hall (far left) housed Vincent Mazzei's shoe repair service on the first floor and a photography studio upstairs. George Hughson's residence was located between Morse Hall and Dr. Francis Robinson's stately Queen Anne-style home—now the Beaverton Bakery. The Stroud Real Estate Office was adjacent to the Oregon Electric track, and the Story residence was just a few blocks away on the far right.

CADY-ANDERSON STORE. The Cady-Anderson store opened around 1905 on Broadway Street. People relied on Cady's to provide dry goods such as beans, baking powder, lard, and spices. Fred Cady purchased produce from local farmers and resold them in his store, often delivering goods to country customers in his wagon. The Beaverton post office was located within the store for a while as well, with Cady serving as postmaster.

MASON CADY'S GENERAL STORE, C. 1910. Mason P. Cady (right), the nephew of Fred Willis Cady, opened a general merchandise store on Broadway Street in 1909 and operated it for four years. In those days, advertisements were often painted directly onto buildings, as seen here with the popular "Monopole" brand of canned goods. Cady also served as mayor of Beaverton in 1917 before moving to Hillsboro to start a career selling automobiles.

BANK OF BEAVERTON. The Bank of Beaverton was just down the street from Mason Cady's general store. Early residents James Mott, John T. Williams, and Benjamin Denney founded the bank in 1910 in a wood-frame building on Broadway Street. From there, it was relocated to the Cady Building at the corner of Watson Street and Farmington Road. In 1923, a Spanish colonial–style building was constructed on Watson Street across from the Cady Building, and the Bank of Beaverton finally moved into its own building. The bank closed in 1934, when it was bought by Jay Gibson of Gaston and reopened as First Security Bank. The building served as a bank until 1964 and has since been the site of a beauty school and an Arthur Miller Dance Studio. It is listed in the National Register of Historic Places.

THE CADY BUILDING. In 1914, Fred Willis Cady built an impressive brick structure at the corner of Watson Street and Farmington Road. It is said to be the first brick building in Beaverton and has come to be known simply as the Cady Building. The building has been occupied by many different businesses over the years, including the Bank of Beaverton, the city library, a post office, and a drugstore. Local dentist Dr. Theodore Hetu shared second-floor office space with Dr. C.E. Mason for many years. Before the Freemasons built their own building on Watson Street in 1936, they used the top floor of the Cady Building for their meetings.

CADY AND PEGG GENERAL MERCHANDISE, C. 1914. The Cady-Anderson store became Cady and Pegg General Merchandise when town undertaker Winfield Pegg bought out Anderson. The new business was on the first floor of the Cady Building on Farmington Road and continued until 1921. The Cady Building, now nearing its 100th birthday, is listed in the National Register of Historic Places.

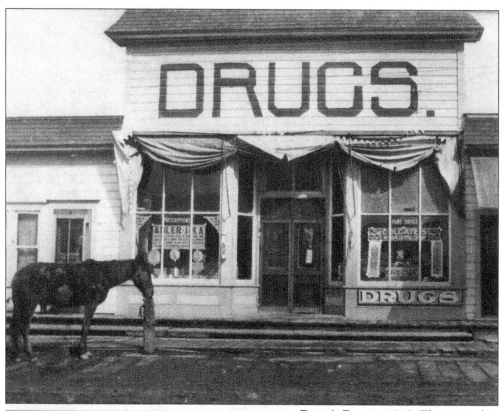

DEAN'S DRUGS, 1915. The original Dean's Drugs was prominently situated on Broadway Street. Much like today, early drug stores sold more than pharmaceuticals, offering sandwiches, cosmetics, tobacco, and soft drinks as well.

DEAN'S DRUGS, 1920S. Dean's Drugs relocated to the ground floor of the Cady Building in the 1920s. Here, Lewis and Mary Dean pose with their son, Harold, in front of their family business in the Cady Building.

CITY OF BEAVERTON, C. 1922. This aerial shot of Beaverton from approximately 1922 shows a town surrounded by farms and a vast rural landscape. Farmington Road bisects the scene horizontally, while Watson Avenue runs north from the town's center into the countryside. The rectangular Cady Building can be seen just south of Farmington Road.

CITY OF BEAVERTON, 1930. Farmington Road again cuts through this photograph horizontally. By 1930, the town was filling in, with many new homes and businesses cropping up. Just left of center is the Cady Building, a Beaverton landmark both then and now.

LIVERMORE SAWMILL. Frank Livermore set up a sawmill on Weir Road near Cooper Mountain in 1896, only to see it burn down just a year later. He rebuilt a little farther north, near what is now 185th Avenue and Hart Road, operating there until 1904. The Livermore Sawmill provided much of the wood for the homes of Beaverton's expanding population. Above, an aproned Esther Livermore stands in the doorway of the second sawmill location. Her three-year-old daughter, Ivy, is on the far right.

LIVERMORE LUMBER COMPANY, C. 1910. In 1904, Frank Livermore bought 280 wooded acres on Cooper Mountain from the railroad company. The land extended to what is now the intersection of Farmington Road and 170th Avenue. He relocated his sawmill for the third time to this location and cleared it of trees over the next five years.

LIVERMORE FARM, 1910. In 1910, Frank Livermore sold his mill and opened a lumberyard near the railroad tracks along Farmington Road. From this location near the rail line, he was able to ship lumber all over the area as well as deliver locally by wagon. The Livermore family lived near the lumberyard in the building that now houses Nona Emilia Italian Restaurant.

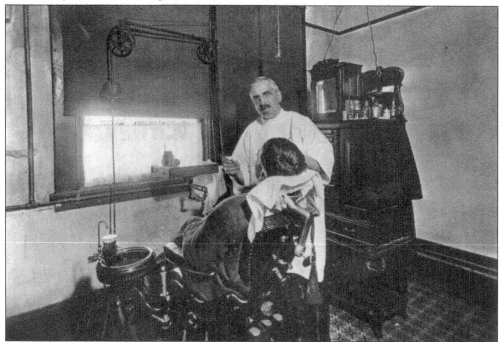

BEAVERTON'S FIRST DENTIST. Originally a barber from Quebec, Canada, Dr. Theodore George Hetu began offering dental services in Beaverton's Cady Building around 1900. His second-floor office was next to Dr. C.E. Mason's, whom he would often assist as an anesthesiologist. When Dr. Hetu's patients had difficulty paying for dental work during the Depression, he often accepted a gift of poultry instead, much to the chagrin of his wife.

ROSE BIGGI AND BEAVERTON FOODS. In 1920, Rose Merlo married a young Italian man named Louie Biggi. They purchased 14 acres of land near today's Cedar Hills Boulevard and began raising horseradish and other vegetables. Rose was widowed just seven years later; suddenly finding herself alone with three children to support, she decided to try her hand at selling her popular homemade ground horseradish, which she sold door-to-door in Hillsboro, Beaverton, and Portland. Her product sold well, and soon her horseradish was known as the best around. Above, Rose poses with Esther, one of the company's first employees, in front of the delivery truck. At right, she poses with a friend at St. Mary's School in 1915. (Both, courtesy of Beaverton Foods.)

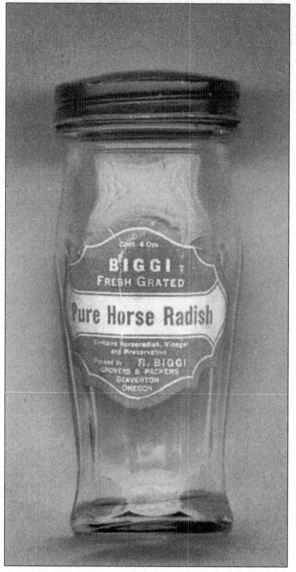

BEAVERTON FOODS LABELS. Although it started as a horseradish company, Rose Biggi's operation soon came to include mustards as well. The condiments were marketed under several different brand names; today, they include Beaver and Inglehoffer. At left is a sample of the first style of glass bottle used by the company. (Both, courtesy of Beaverton Foods.)

First Processing Location, Rose Biggi's Basement, Beaverton, Oregon 1929

BEAVERTON HORSERADISH FACTORY. Rose Biggi operated her fledgling condiment business out of her basement while she saved up money to buy additional land and build a larger house (below). Today, Beaverton Foods is still a family-run business and is the largest producer of non-refrigerated horseradish and mustards in the country. The company headquarters have relocated to Hillsboro, but Rose Merlo's 1929 venture into the condiment business remains a timeless Beaverton success story. (Both, courtesy of Beaverton Foods.)

INTERIOR OF THYNG'S CONFECTIONERY. George Thyng was born in 1873 in Reedville, a small town west of Beaverton that is now part of Aloha. He married his wife, Lillian, in 1909. Thyng's Confectionery was located adjacent to the Cady-Anderson store on Broadway Street. In addition to running the store, George served as the city's first city recorder, was the deputy registrar for a time, and was a justice of the peace. In the above image, George Thyng and Archie Masters pose inside the confectionery in the early 1900s. Below, from left to right, are George, his brother Herbert Thyng, and Ray Alberts.

THYNG'S CONFECTIONERY, 1920S. Below, from left to right, Harry Barnes, Wallace Brown, Roy Berst, and Ed Brown pose in front of the confectionery on Broadway Street. Thyng's Confectionery was more than a candy store; Lillian Thyng operated the telephone exchange on the back wall, the first of its kind in Beaverton. Rossi's Saloon is on the left. (Above, courtesy of Beaverton High School.)

Monopole Canned Goods

20TH CENTURY GROCERY

Prices in this store are abso-

lutely the same as our Port-

land store

Beaverton   Oregon

ON THE HIGHWAY

20TH CENTURY STORE. This building at the corner of Hall Boulevard and Broadway Street was called the 20th Century Store and the Thrifty Market at different times during its years as a grocery store. It has also been the home of a blueprinting business and a hardware store. Today, the Beaverton Historical Society calls this historic building home. (Above, courtesy of Beaverton High School.)

Main Street of Beaverton

THE FISHER BUILDING. Earl Fisher played many roles in early Beaverton—teacher, newspaper editor, and five-time mayor. He is also credited with constructing the brick building on Broadway Street bearing his name. The two-story building was built in 1916, with a west wing added in 1921. Fisher operated the *Owl* newspaper from his office in this building. The ground floor once housed a bus depot as well as the Beaver Inn and the White Hall Restaurant, while the second story was rented out as office space. The upper floor was the location of Dr. Talbert's dental practice and Dr. Welch's medical practice for more than 50 years. When Fisher encountered financial difficulties, he sold the building to the Rossi family. Today, it is part of the Beaverton Downtown Historic District and is listed in the National Register of Historic Places. It is still home to a wide array of businesses.

BROADWAY AT WEST STREET. A man pauses in front of a building on Broadway at West Street. This building was razed to make room for Elmer Stipe's garage in the early 1920s, and later Guy Carr's dealership.

MUESSIG'S FLOUR MILL, C. 1920. Albert Muessig's flour mill was located at Farmington Road and Cedar Hills Boulevard. "Before buying flour and feed come and get our prices—we can save you money" claims an advertisement painted directly onto the building, as was common in the early part of the 20th century. The Muessig family home can be seen in the background at right. Part of the Muessig flour mill was used as a cannery as late as the 1960s.

"THE TRAIL OF VENGEANCE"
Featuring
AL FERGUSON & PAULINE CURLEY

PREMIUM PICTURES, 1920s. Beaverton became a minor player in the silent film industry when Dr. G.E. Watts and four other Portland businessmen founded the 32-acre Premium Pictures film studio in 1922. In the stock photograph above, the actors in 1924's *The Trail of Vengeance* pose in front of a log building on Erickson Street. This log building was used in a subsequent film as well, in which it was burned down as part of the plot. Local Beaverton residents often played small parts as extras in these films, which were usually shown to a full house at the theater, with proceeds benefiting local organizations like the fire department.

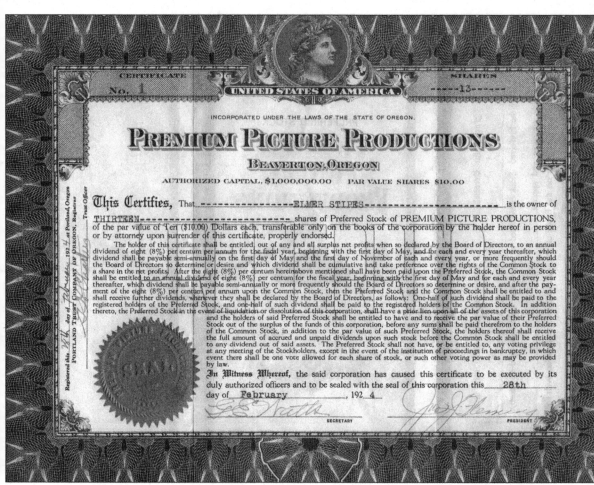

PREMIUM PICTURES STOCK. Partners Dr. G.E.Watts and J.J.Fleming raised money for the construction of the film studio by selling stock to local residents. The main building on Erickson Street was 400 feet long and had a roof more than 30 feet high. It was used as an indoor filming location for silent films featuring a heroic Al Ferguson rescuing various damsels in distress. The film studio produced approximately 15 silent films including *Crashing Courage, Flames of Passion, The Frame-up, The Power Drive, Scars of Hate, The Vow of Vengeance, The Way of the Transgressor, Harbor Patrol,* and *Shackles of Fear.* By 1924, however, the studio had run out of money and had to close its doors.

Three

EDUCATION

Beaverton School District No. 48 has been in operation since July 1960, but schools operated in the area for more than 100 years before that date. The very first schools were known as subscription schools, as they were paid for by donations from individual families and were usually housed in people's homes or in small one-room cabins. As the population grew, small school districts began to form and their schools were referred to as common schools, as they were open to all and supported by public funds. Any discrepancies between funds provided and expenses incurred were made up with donations from students' families.

Between 1856 and 1960, there were 16 individual districts in the Beaverton area—later reduced to 13 through consolidation—more than half of which operated just one school each. Unification of these small, individual districts was discussed as early as 1925, but it was not until the 1950s that population growth and changing expectations of common standards brought the idea of unification to the table again.

In 1955, a committee put together by the Union High School District expressed the desire for a junior high school, and unification was seen as the best way to implement the model. The push for a single unified school district was helped along by the Oregon legislature when House Bill 163 passed in August 1957. The new law required that all Oregon counties organize their schools into districts within 12 years, and Beaverton Unified School District No. 48 was established just three years later, on July 1, 1960. At that time, the district was approximately 57 square miles and contained 20 elementary schools, 2 high schools, and 11,418 students in grades 1–12.

LITTLE KNOWLEDGE BOX. The earliest pioneer children usually attended classes in their own log home or at a neighbor's. Sometimes, if the population supported it, small schoolhouses were erected on private land, such as the one above, dubbed the "Little Knowledge Box."

SCHOLLS FERRY SCHOOL, C. 1890. The one-room Scholls Ferry schoolhouse attracted students from miles around. Attendance was often sporadic, however, as many children—especially boys—were needed to help on family farms. (Courtesy of Judy Donovan.)

PROGRESS/MCKAY SCHOOL. Known first as the Betts Schools, after the name of the schoolmaster, then as the Progress School, due to its location in the Progress area of Augustus Fanno's land, it became the McKay School when a new, larger building was constructed on James McKay's donated land claim in 1865. (Both, courtesy of Judy Donovan.)

PROGRESS/McKAY SCHOOL, 1914. The early schoolhouses often provided a basic education to several children from the same family, with all ages attending together, as shown in this 1914 photograph of the McKay School student body. (Courtesy of Judy Donovan.)

COOPER MOUNTAIN SCHOOL, 1905. Cooper Mountain School opened in 1892 with 16 students and remained a very small school for most of its history; in 1947, it still had just 56 children attending. The student body in 1905 included, from left to right, (first row) Ivy Livermore, Clem Kemmer, Susie Kemmer, Fred Reusser, Eva Kemmer, and Edna Reusser; (back row) unidentified, teacher Ivy Peterson, unidentified, and Bertha Reusser.

FIRST BEAVERTON SCHOOL. After much debate about its location, the first official school in Beaverton was constructed in 1874. On Broadway Street in an area known as the "Beaverton Ditch," it was encircled by a six-foot fence with a turnstile serving a dual purpose—to keep kids in and livestock out. The inclusion of this fence was written into the sales contract between the district and James and Mary Steel, who sold the land to the school district for $50 in gold coin. Should the fence be taken down, or the schoolchildren trespass on the Steel property, the whole contract was null and void and the land would revert to the Steels. Today, a large Bed Bath & Beyond store occupies the site of Beaverton's first school.

BEAVERTON SCHOOL. The Beaverton School was heated by a potbellied stove and had no plumbing. As the population grew, so did the little school. A second classroom was built in 1884, and a third added in 1895. By 1900, it was clear that a new, larger facility was needed. Above, the class of 1902 gathers for a group photograph.

BEAVERTON SCHOOL, 1910. The Beaverton School was in use until 1910, when the burgeoning student population necessitated a larger facility. When the new building was finished and ready for students, a photographer was brought in to take photographs of the last classes to attend the old school. Above is the last class of grades 7–10 to attend the school, and below is the last class of grades 4–6.

BEAVERTON PUBLIC SCHOOL. In 1910, a four-room, two-story building was constructed on Second Street between Stott and Erickson Streets. It was considered state-of-the-art for the times, as it had a full basement and the latest heating devices, although it did not have a direct water line until 1913. When it opened in January 1911, students marched through town carrying their books and supplies to relocate to the new school. It was known as the Beaverton Public School, like its predecessor, and then as Beaverton Grade School after a high school was built in 1916. The above image shows the 1924 addition to the rear of the building.

BEAVERTON GRADE SCHOOL, 1924–1925. The Beaverton Grade School did not pass its 1935 inspection. Although fire escapes had been added to the top floor, the building was deemed a fire hazard due to its narrow furnace ventilation shaft and exposed wiring. There were also not enough restrooms and the lighting was inadequate. It was decided that, once again, a larger, newer building was needed. Part of the funds for a new facility were provided by the government through the Works Progress Administration, and the remaining money was raised through a bond election. The old building was razed in 1938 after the new school was built nearby at the corner of Farmington Road and Erickson Avenue (now the Merle Davies Annex of Beaverton High School). Today, the east wing of Beaverton High School stands where the Beaverton Grade School once stood.

BEAVERTON HIGH SCHOOL. In 1915, the school board asked voters to approve $21,000 for a 21-room high school even though there were only 21 high school students at the time. Many people opposed the proposal and protested against it, but the fact that there were 150 students at the grade school was not lost on the majority of voters, and the bond was approved. The foresight of the 1915 voters was rewarded shortly thereafter: the high school population doubled during the 1915–1916 school year, and again the following year. By 1920, there were 96 high school students. More classrooms were added in 1929 to accommodate the school's 274 students, and again throughout the 1950s, as the student body soared closer to 1,000.

RALEIGH HILLS SCHOOL, 1912. Raleigh Hills was named for early resident Raleigh Robinson. The first schoolhouse in the Raleigh Hills area was a one-room building built in 1893, which served 25 students in its opening year. The student population at Raleigh Hills School remained low—under 30 students most years—until after World War II, when it finally saw its population increase dramatically. Minnie Davis is the teacher in this 1912 photograph.

BEAVERTON HIGH SCHOOL BASKETBALL, 1913. Beaverton's first girls' basketball team included, from left to right, Amy Squires, Helen Baird, Margaret Jones, Kathryn Desinger, Alice Watts, Mary Shepard, Coach J.E. Wagoner, Margaret Peterson, Goldie Vincent, Azalea Young, Rita Fitzpatrick, Hazel Pegg, and Anna Peterson.

BEAVERTON HIGH SCHOOL, 1913. Students at the high school in 1913 included, from left to right, (first row) Ildrie King, Pauline West, Wilbur Warhman, Willis Cady, and Arthur Jones; (second row) Bramwell Price, Margaret Jones, Kathryn Desinger, Amy Snider, Amy Squires, Alice Watts, and Harry Barnes; (third row) Leon Davis, Frank Kline, Azalea Young, Goldie Vincent, Anna Peterson, Helen Baird, and Pearl Hughson; (fourth row) Arthur Allen, Pansy Smith, Vallie Stitt, Laura Zinibrick, Mary Shepard, Margaret Peterson, Hazel Pegg, and teacher J.E. Wagoner; (top center) Lester Jones.

1912 GRADUATION. "Onward Is Our Aim" was a popular class motto in the first half of the 1900s, gracing many graduation banners and pamphlets. In 1912, Beaverton graduates chose the motto to commemorate the end of their high school years.

BEAVERTON HIGH SCHOOL SOUVENIRS. Since opening its doors in 1916, Beaverton High School has been a school of longstanding traditions. From its earliest days, students received souvenirs upon graduation as well as ribbons and memorabilia from sports games and school functions. Spirit ribbons were printed up for home and away games, often highlighting parts of school cheers or songs. This friendly competitiveness still contributes to a sense of allegiance and camaraderie among the student body. (Courtesy of Judy Donovan.)

AERIAL VIEW OF BEAVERTON HIGH SCHOOL. Beaverton High School stands out near the center of this early photograph. When it first opened in 1916, one-third of the funds needed to operate the school came from tuition paid by students outside the district who did not have a high school to attend in their own area.

BEAVERTON HIGH SCHOOL BUSES, 1920s. Beaverton began using touring cars to bus students to Beaverton High School in 1925. The first school bus was put into use at the start of the 1925 school year. It was bought from Otto Erickson's Garage and driven by one of his stepsons, Lee Carr. Many residents opposed the busing of out-of-district students until they learned that the students were bringing in tuition that more than paid for the buses.

BEAVERTON HIGH SCHOOL FLEET, 1920s. By 1928, there were five vehicles in the Beaverton fleet, and elementary school students benefitted from the transportation option as well. (Courtesy of Beaverton High School.)

BEAVERTON SCHOOL BUS, 1930s. A school bus from Beaverton fills up at the pump before filling up with school children. By 1931, Beaverton was operating eight buses and was switching to the new all-metal construction instead of the carriage-like touring cars. After the reorganization of the school districts into one district in 1960, a bus garage was built on Allen Avenue to house and maintain the school district's fleet.

BEAVERTON HIGH SCHOOL BASKETBALL TEAMS, 1927–1928. Beaverton High School has had both boys' and girls' basketball teams since its earliest days. Below, the girls' team brings some swashbuckling fun to the sport in this 1928 team photograph. (Both, courtesy of Beaverton High School.)

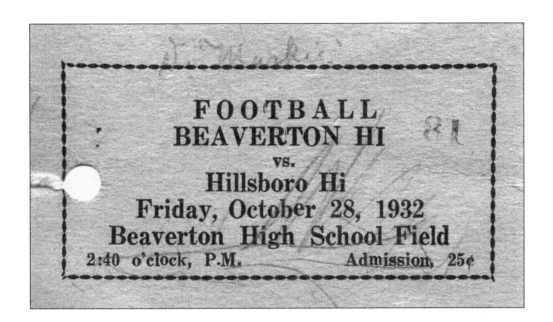

FOOTBALL
BEAVERTON HI
vs.
Hillsboro Hi
Friday, October 28, 1932
Beaverton High School Field

2:40 o'clock, P.M.   Admission, 25¢

BEAVERTON HIGH SCHOOL FOOTBALL. As with most high schools, football brings out the competitiveness and the school spirit in the student body. The football team played regularly against other area high schools, usually filling the seats at the Friday night games. The black-and-orange-clad Beavers of Beaverton High School continue the tradition today, with both freshman and JV teams. (Above, courtesy of Judy Donovan; below, courtesy of Beaverton High School.)

BACCALAUREATE SERVICES

Class of 1927

BEAVERTON HIGH SCHOOL

Prelude   *"Pilgrim's Chorus"*   Wagner
       BETHEL ORCHESTRA

Hymn

Invocation
       REV. J. FRANK CUNNINGHAM

Anthem   *"Goin' Home"*   Dvorak
    HIGH SCHOOL GIRLS' GLEE CLUB

Scripture Reading,
       REV. J. FRANK CUNNINGHAM

Anthem   *"Invictus"*   Huhn
    HIGH SCHOOL BOYS' GLEE CLUB

Address   Dr. J. F. Dobbs
    PRESIDENT PACIFIC UNIVERSITY

Benediction

BACCALAUREATE PROGRAM, 1927. Commencement ceremonies have always been an important part of senior year. At Beaverton High School, students have always been honored with a more somber Baccalaureate service in addition to the festive celebrations of graduation. (Courtesy of Beaverton High School.)

BEAVERTON HIGH SCHOOL FIRE SQUAD, 1935–1936. The fire squad, established in 1922, was a group of volunteer students whose job it was to conduct fire drills and promote greater efficiency during evacuations. During the 1935–1936 school year, the standing record was an impressive 54 seconds to evacuate the entire building. (Courtesy of Beaverton High School.)

SENIOR PLAY, 1937. The high school put on two plays each year—one by the senior class and one by the student body association. In 1937, the senior play was *Believe It Or Not*, a comedy directed by Geraldine Sanford. (Courtesy of Beaverton High School.)

BEAVERTON HIGH SCHOOL BAND, 1937. The 32-member band played at many school and community functions, but the trip to Eugene to participate in the state band contest was the highlight of the year in 1937. They also participated annually in the Portland Rose Festival and Beaverton's Junior Parade. (Both, courtesy of Beaverton High School.)

Four

PLANES, TRAINS,
AND AUTOMOBILES

Before 1850, the only route from the Beaverton area to Portland was an Indian trail that meandered—often through mud—over the steep West Hills Canyon. A plank road was begun in 1851 to link the young town with Portland, but its construction suffered stops and starts and was not completed until the early 1860s. Once the plank road was in place, it helped to triple Beaverton's population and was a boon to the economy as it became much easier to transport goods from the farms of the valley to the merchants of Portland.

The railway was the next step in Beaverton's transportation evolution. The Oregon Central Railroad Company had agreed to build a depot in town if there was at least one commercial building nearby to warrant it. George Betts promptly built a log building at the corner of Farmington Road and Angel Street, declared it a store, and the depot was built. The first steam train rolled into the station in 1871, confirming Beaverton as a "whistle stop" on the expanding route map.

Electric train service inevitably followed. The interurban Oregon Electric Railway completed its Portland-to-Salem route in early 1908, and an extension to Beaverton and points west was in service by the end of 1909. Travel by electric train was convenient, relatively fast, and at about 3¢ per mile, fairly economical. The trains were popular and allowed people to live in Beaverton and work or sell their goods in the larger cities of Portland and Salem.

Not to be outdone, the competing rail company, Southern Pacific, began its "Red Electric" service to Beaverton in 1914. Both companies operated their electric train service until the end of the 1920s, when competition from the automobile forced them to cease passenger service. Today, however, Beaverton's train service has been resurrected, having evolved into the Portland Westside MAX light-rail line that offers commuters a quick, reliable, and car-free way to get from Beaverton to Portland. Several sections of the MAX light-rail line are located along the former Oregon Electric's right-of-ways.

OREGON ELECTRIC RAILWAY CREW. The Oregon Electric Company began service between Portland and Salem in 1907 and began construction on the Beaverton line in 1908. It branched off at Garden Home and offered service to Beaverton, Hillsboro, and eventually Forest Grove. Round-trip tickets between Beaverton and Portland could be purchased for 50¢, although many commuters purchased booklets for multiple trips. (Below, courtesy of Judy Donovan.)

This cover is good for the 50th trip.

SOUTHERN PACIFIC COMPANY—PACIFIC SYSTEM	1900 AND

NON-TRANSFERABLE FIFTY TRIP COMMUTATION TICKET
Good for Fifty (50) Single Trips *without stop-over between*

PORTLAND (E) and RALEIGH

Void after date punched in margin.

Subject to conditions printed hereon, to which the purchaser hereby in writing assents

Issued to M ____ *Mary Vose* ____
Sign in ink—Do not use pencil   Purchaser.

No Baggage Privileges.   **Form 323**

Passenger Traffic Manager

641

2	21
22	23
JAN.	JULY
FEB.	AUG.
MAR.	SEPT.
APR.	OCT.
MAY	NOV.
JUNE	DEC.

Day | 2 | 4 | 6 | 8 | 10 | 12 | 14 | 16 | 18 | 20 | 22 | 24 | 26 | 28 | 30
1 | 3 | 5 | 7 | 9 | 11 | 13 | 15 | 17 | 19 | 21 | 23 | 25 | 27 | 29 | 31

OREGON ELECTRIC RAILWAY DEPOT. Above, the Oregon Electric Beaverton depot (1) was located near the city's first schoolhouse (2). By 1913, the depot had been enlarged to accommodate the increase in rail travel and had received new siding and a loading platform. The trains ran on electricity and offered quieter, cleaner, and more dependable service than the steam-powered trains. They allowed residents of the more rural Tualatin Valley to travel relatively quickly to Portland for business or recreation. Below, Laura Walker Olds, the granddaughter of early settler William Walker, waits in a buggy beside the upgraded and enlarged depot.

CHANGE IN PASSENGER TRAIN SCHEDULES

THURSDAY, MAY 11TH

Oregon Electric Railway

On the date named above changes in time will be made on trains as outlined below:

From Portland

Train No. 33, leaving Portland 7:45 a. m. for Forest Grove and intermediate points, will make all stops between Portland and Garden Home in addition to those west of Garden Home.

Train No. 53, leaving Portland at 7:50 a. m. for Garden Home, will be discontinued.

Train No. 55 for Tualatin, leaving Portland 9:45 a. m., will run daily instead of daily except Sunday.

Train No. 7, leaving Portland 10:45 a. m. for Corvallis, will arrive Albany 1:45 instead of 1:55, Corvallis 2:10 instead of 2:20. Will not make stops Sundays between Garden Home and Tualatin.

Train No. 59, leaving Portland 3:05 p. m. for Garden Home, will run daily instead of daily except Sunday.

Train No. 61 will leave Portland 3:35 p. m. instead of 3:55 for Tualatin.

Train No. 63, leaving Portland 5:00 p. m. for Tualatin, will run daily instead of daily except Sunday.

Train No. 65 will leave Portland 5:35 p. m. instead of 5:40 for Tualatin and Tonquin.

Train No. 17 will leave Portland 6:05 p. m. instead of 6:25 for Salem.

Train No. 67, leaving Portland 11:20 p. m. for Wilsonville, will run through to Salem, Saturdays, arriving Salem 1:20 a. m.

Arriving Portland

Trains Nos. 52 and 58, arriving Portland 7:25 a. m. and 11:45 a. m. from Tualatin, will run daily instead of daily except Sunday.

Train No. 6, arriving Portland 8:25 a. m. from Salem, will make local stops between Garden Home and Portland.

Train No. 56, now arriving Portland 9:30 a. m. from Garden Home, will be discontinued.

Train No. 10 will arrive Portland 11:30 a. m. instead of 11:35, from Eugene, and will not make local stops Sunday between Tualatin and Portland.

Train No. 12 will arrive Portland 1:15 p. m. instead of 1:20 from Salem.

Train No. 62, arriving Portland 4:30 p. m. from Garden Home, will run daily instead of daily except Sunday.

Train No. 64 will leave Tualatin 4:40 p. m. instead of 5:07, arrive Portland 5:30 p. m. instead of 6:00.

Train No. 20, arriving Portland 7:40 p. m., will make local stops between Tualatin and Metzger.

Train No. 22 will leave Eugene 5:20 p. m. instead of 5:25, Albany 6:50 instead of 7:00, Salem 7:50 instead of 7:55, arrive Portland 9:50 instead of 10:05.

The leaving and arriving time quoted above is at North Bank Station; the time of trains at Jefferson Street Station is 15 minutes later leaving Portland and 15 minutes earlier arriving.

Reduced round trip fares in effect daily to Garden Home and all points south and west thereof, return limit 7 days.

OREGON ELECTRIC'S OBSERVATION CAR. The observation cars of the Oregon Electric Railway were designed with the passengers' comfort in mind. The floors were carpeted, the seats plush, and the mahogany trim polished. The ceilings were painted in an elegant green and gold. The Oregon Electric was a very popular means of transportation; by 1909, there were 38 cars in the fleet and they were always crowded. Fares were 3¢ per mile, with an extra fee charged to ride in the opulent observation car. (Left, courtesy of Judy Donovan.)

SOUTHERN PACIFIC DEPOT, 1920S. The Southern Pacific cut through old downtown, carrying passengers and products such as vegetables, lumber, and timber. Above, Farmington Road can be seen on the right and Broadway Street is on the left, with the depot in the center. Below, the urban progressiveness of the train depot contrasts with the rural, agrarian landscape of early Beaverton.

Southern Pacific Service Shop. Southern Pacific's Red Electric trains came to Beaverton in 1914, giving passengers an alternative to the Oregon Electric line. The rail company opened service shops along Fifth Street to provide local repair services for their trains. These bright red coaches with their unique round windows were a popular and efficient way to get around. Southern Pacific enjoyed a 15-year period of lucrative business with its electric trains, offering an east-side route that took passengers to Sherwood and Tualatin, and a west-side route connecting Forest Grove, Hillsboro, and Beaverton. With the advent of the personal automobile, however, passenger train service began to suffer dwindling patronage. By 1931, the Red Electric train service had ceased operations, and most of the track was dismantled by the following year. Here, several local service shop workers pose for a photograph outside their Fifth Street shop.

"STIPER" AIRPLANE, 1930s. Elmer Stipe was the first Chevrolet dealer in Beaverton. George Yates, his friend and business partner, was a pilot who came to Beaverton after World War I and began designing and building gliders and airplanes at the 33-acre Watts Airport along Erickson Street, where the then-defunct Premium Pictures had been located. Yates designed this two-seater airplane for Stipe using a modified Chevrolet engine called the Martin 333. The plane was known as the "Stiper" and flew a total of about 4,000 hours. When the airplane-design business outgrew Watts Airport, operations were moved to a strip of land along Cedar Hills Boulevard owned by Charles Bernard. The Bernard Airport, as it came to be known, thrived for many years and gained the distinction of being the oldest continuously operated airport in the state.

BERNARD AIRPORT. Charles Bernard's airfield was the testing ground for several types of experimental aircraft throughout the 1930s. This was before the industry became highly regulated, so aviation enthusiasts like George Yates, Marvin Joy, and Johnny Bigelow were free to explore different types of aircraft body and wing positions. Joy even created a wingless airplane, which managed to get into the air just briefly on two occasions. The plane below was Yates's design and featured a lattice-style geodetic construction, which made it much stronger than the typical airplane of the day. (Both, courtesy of the Washington County Historical Museum.)

BEAVERTON AIRPORT, 1966. By the late 1960s, the airport was surrounded by commercial and residential properties, and Charles Bernard could no longer afford the high taxes on the land. In 1969, after nearly 40 years in operation, the hangars were demolished and sold to a developer who wanted the land for a shopping mall. Charles Bernard himself drove the bulldozer that razed the airport. This aerial shot looks north along Cedar Hills Boulevard. Cedar Hills Crossing shopping mall now occupies the site.

OTTO ERICKSON'S GARAGE. Swedish immigrant Otto Erickson ventured into the automobile business when he settled in Beaverton in 1912. He bought out the only Ford dealership in Washington County, in Sherwood, and moved it to Beaverton. His initial $3,500 investment had grown to an impressive $96,000 by 1920, and by the early 1920s, Erickson had become the Ford agent for all of Washington County. His shop was conveniently located adjacent to the railroad tracks near Farmington Road, so when the Ford cars arrived unassembled it was quick work to unload, assemble, and sell them to urban and rural families around the county. In front of the service shop are, from left to right, Howard Boyd, Guy Carr (Erickson's stepson), Otto Erickson, Ralph Snipe, and Speedy Classen.

OTTO ERICKSON'S BLACKSMITH SHOP, C. 1915. In the early 1900s, parts were not yet readily available for cars, so it was still necessary to have a blacksmith nearby to manufacture needed replacements. Otto Erickson's blacksmith shop was located at Farmington Road and Main Street, just down the street from his dealership. "Do not ask for credit," warns a sign on the wall. As president of his company, Erickson owned 80 percent of the company's stock, spreading the remaining 20 percent among his employees as a reward for loyal service, and paying them a generous 75¢ per hour. His employees also doubled as salesmen, and received $35 for each car they sold. In the 1923 photograph below are, from left to right, George Lichty, Cecil Barnes, James Whitworth, Joe Muessig, and Guy Carr.

OTTO ERICKSON. Although Otto Erickson, shown here with a 1920 Ford Model T, was a savvy businessman, his Ford business experienced tough times in the late 1920s. Much of this could be attributed to the onset of the Great Depression, and the fact that the Model A was coming out and people were no longer interested in the older Model T. Erickson had to sell off his remaining stock of Model Ts at a loss. The burning of his Beaverton Garage in 1934 or 1935 brought the then-struggling business to an end. (Left, courtesy of Beaverton High School.)

ANDREW KENNEDY ON HIS MAIL ROUTE, C. 1915. Andrew Kennedy favored his Brush car, as did many mail carriers in the early days of automobiles, because of its simplicity and relatively low cost. It was also relatively easy to fix since it ran on just one cylinder.

CARR'S CAR SERVICE, 1930S. Guy Carr operated this service shop on Broadway Street and Watson Avenue during the difficult years of the Depression. Times were tough and people were not buying many cars, so Carr sold gas and operated a school bus and a tow truck out of this building. However, sometimes even the city could not pay him for his services and often issued IOUs instead.

STIPE'S GARAGE, 1920s. Elmer Stipe opened his Chevrolet business in 1921 a few years after his water company went bankrupt. The building was located on the southwest end of Broadway Street, and was supposedly modeled after a similarly styled garage in Seaside, Oregon. In 1940, the building was sold to Guy Carr, who remodeled it and continued to sell cars from this location. Today, the building is used by Beaverton Kia.

CARR CHEVROLET, 1942. Stipe's Garage became Johnson's Garage, and eventually Carr Chevrolet when Guy Carr bought it in 1940. Carr had bought out his stepfather's Beaverton car business in 1923 and continued operating it until it burned down in 1930. Not one to be discouraged, Guy Carr opened several other car dealerships in various Beaverton locations, including the former Stipe's Garage. Today, Carr Chevrolet continues to thrive at its current location on Canyon Road.

Five

RELIGIOUS LIFE

The first religious gatherings were held in the log homes of early settlers. As the population grew, community "camp meetings" began to be held near present-day Scholls Ferry Road. Attendees sat on log benches brought in from the sawmills on Fanno Creek. These meetings not only provided a time and place for early residents to gather for worship, but also allowed them to mingle with neighbors who often lived miles away.

In 1853, land belonging to James Davies at present-day Scholls Ferry and Hall Boulevard was chosen as a more permanent location for a church. The lumber was prepared at the Denney Sawmill and the tongue-and-groove Ames Chapel was in use later that year. Services were provided by circuit riders and people came from miles around to attend. The congregation of Ames Chapel was Methodist Episcopal, reflecting the fact that Washington County was predominantly Protestant until near the end of the century. By 1889, Methodists, Adventists, and Congregationalists all had houses of worship in Beaverton.

The first Catholic community in Beaverton was the Sisters of the Most Precious Blood, an order relocated from Sublimity, Oregon, which began serving in an orphanage in Beaverton in 1891. In 1905, they changed their name to the Sisters of St. Mary. A priest traveled into Beaverton to say Mass at a converted cheese factory until a permanent Catholic facility was built in 1913. The new building included a basement used for social gatherings and an upper floor with four rooms used as classrooms. This new parish was named St. Cecilia's and the congregation worshiped in this building until 1949, when it moved to its current location on Franklin Street.

Ames Chapel is no longer, but its burying ground was renamed Crescent Grove and expanded over the years. The old cemetery lies just off Greenburg Road near Washington Square Mall and is the final resting place for many of Beaverton's earliest residents, including the Fannos, Spencers, McKays, Denneys, Robinsons, Stotts, and Tuckers.

ST. MARY'S HOME FOR BOYS, 1904. In 1889, archbishop William H. Gross requested that an orphanage be built about a mile outside the town of Beaverton. The orphanage opened in 1891, and within a month, housed 60 children. A rail stop called St. Mary's was added in order to connect the remote location to town. (Courtesy of the Sisters of St. Mary of Oregon.)

ST. MARY'S HOME FOR BOYS, 1923. When it opened in 1891, the home was open to both boys and girls. Later, the girls were relocated to St. Mary's Home for Girls in St. Paul, Oregon, and boys under the age of six were sent to Portland for care. Father Heesaker poses here with the graduating class of 1923. (Courtesy of St. Cecilia's Parish.)

SISTERS OF ST. MARY MOTHERHOUSE. The motherhouse, less than half a mile from the orphanage, was completed in early 1894. The top floor was reserved for dormitories, while the first floor contained a music studio, parlor, dining room, and community room. On the second floor, a beautiful chapel spanned the entire length of the front of the building. (Courtesy of the Sisters of St. Mary of Oregon.)

THE SISTERS, 1890S. The order's original name, Sisters of the Most Precious Blood, was carved prominently into the entryway of the motherhouse. The name was changed to the Sisters of St. Mary's in 1905. It cost a lot to operate the new motherhouse as well as the school, and for the first several years, the sisters operated at a loss financially, resorting to growing and selling onions to supplement their meager incomes. (Courtesy of the Sisters of St. Mary of Oregon.)

INTERIOR OF THE MOTHERHOUSE CHAPEL. The chapel on the second floor of St. Mary's Institute was much loved by the sisters. It extended the entire length of the front of the building and provided a quiet space for worship and reflection. Many of the sisters lamented having to abandon this cherished chapel when they moved to a new facility in the 1930s. Fortunately, they were able to bring a piece of it with them, as the beautiful stained glass windows were saved and installed in the chapel of the new motherhouse. (Courtesy of the Sisters of St. Mary of Oregon.)

ST. MARY'S INSTITUTE. Wings were added on both the western and eastern sides of the motherhouse when the sisters outgrew the smaller building. The sisters continued to live in the building as well as operate the school and boardinghouse while starting to scout for a new location that would allow for expansion.

ST. MARY'S SCHOOL, 1906. The convent, where the sisters lived and operated the school, is on the right, and the orphanage is on the left. The buildings were damaged by a chimney fire in 1930, making the need for a larger and safer facility a top priority.

ST. MARY'S INSTITUTE, 1909. St. Mary's Institute was filled to capacity within just two years of opening. A 60-acre piece of land, just south of the railroad tracks, caught the eye of the archbishop and the sisters as a good site for a future school. It belonged to George Hornbuckle and was part of a large tract of land known as Hornbuckle Estate. (Courtesy of the Sisters of St. Mary of Oregon.)

CONVENT CONSTRUCTION, 1930. The land for a new convent was purchased from George Hornbuckle in 1903 at a cost of $4,000. Hornbuckle was sure that the sisters would not be able to afford the large acreage and wrongly thought that he would be able to buy it back at a profit within a few years. In March 1930, construction of the new convent began, and in September of that year, the sisters moved into the new facilities. (Courtesy of the Sisters of St. Mary of Oregon.)

CONSTRUCTION OF THE EAST WING, 1951. Within 20 years of its construction, the convent was in need of expansion. An east wing was built, shown in this view from the southeast corner of the property. The sisters were resourceful, using the land behind the convent to grow vegetables. The field is now bisected by Murray Boulevard. (Courtesy of the Sisters of St. Mary of Oregon.)

ST. CECILIA'S CATHOLIC CHURCH AND SCHOOL, 1913. Early Beaverton residents had to travel to Cedar Mill to attend Mass at St. Anthony's, as the first Beaverton Mass was not said until 1908. The Archdiocese bought a piece of land in 1903 near the intersection of Canyon Road and Hall Boulevard and moved an old cheese factory onto it to serve as a parish building. Father Patrick James O'Flynn served as pastor from 1912 until 1917. (Both, courtesy of St. Cecilia's Parish.)

St. Cecilia's, c. 1913. In 1913, the old cheese factory was demolished and an official church building was constructed on the site. The new church accommodated about 75 people, with rooms on the upper level serving as the school, and the basement used as a social hall. An Italian immigrant family, the Reghittos, donated the church bell. Damerow Ford now spans the block where St. Cecilia's once stood. (Courtesy of St. Cecilia's Parish.)

St. Cecilia's Rectory. In 1915, the parish house in Cedar Mill burned to the ground. A new rectory was built next to the church, providing the priests of St. Cecilia's a more spacious and closer place to live. The rectory building still stands in downtown Beaverton as the rear section of the Bike Gallery. (Courtesy of St. Cecilia's Parish.)

ST. CECILIA'S PARISH UNDER CONSTRUCTION, 1948. Father O'Keefe was appointed to St. Cecilia's in 1935. Seeing that the parish was outgrowing its facilities but denied money for land by the archdiocese, O'Keefe bought about three blocks of land a little farther south, spending $1,000 of his own money. He sold off lots until he recouped his investment and donated the remaining parcel of land to the church. (Courtesy of St. Cecilia's Parish.)

DEDICATION OF ST. CECILIA'S PARISH, 1949. Construction on a new church building began in 1948 and the 500-seat church was ready in the spring of 1949. Archbishop Edward D. Howard officiated at the dedication ceremony in the fall of that year. The statue of St. Cecilia was the only remnant of the old building to be incorporated into the new one. (Courtesy of St. Cecilia's Parish.)

METHODIST CHURCH, C. 1900. Before the Methodists had a facility of their own in Beaverton, they worshipped in the Congregationalist church. In 1885, William Hocken donated land to the Methodists and a church was erected that same year at the corner of Fourth Street and Watson Avenue. It was a small one-room building heated by a potbellied stove. When the original building was razed to make way for a new church, the stained glass was saved and made into souvenirs for the parishioners.

COMMUNITY CHURCH PICNIC. Camaraderie among different denominations was the norm among the city's early residents. In the group photograph above, Beaverton's Congregationalists, Methodists, and Adventists gather for a community Sunday school picnic around 1889 at First Street and Front Street (now Farmington Road). Below, Beaverton's Methodists and Congregationalists gather together in 1913. The two religious affiliations shared a building until the Methodists built their own place of worship in 1885.

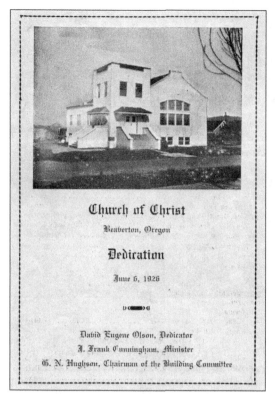

Church of Christ

Beaverton, Oregon

Dedication

June 6, 1926

David Eugene Olson, Dedicator
J. Frank Cunningham, Minister
G. N. Hughson, Chairman of the Building Committee

BEAVERTON CHRISTIAN CHURCH. Originally called the Beaverton Church of Christ, this building was erected at the corner of Second Street and Main Avenue in 1926. The congregation first met in a tent on the site, and then in the Beaver Theater on Broadway Street while awaiting the opening of their own facility. The congregation, under the direction of their first minister, J. Frank Cunningham, grew in number from just 65 in the summer of 1925 to 120 when the new building opened a year later. The congregation moved into its present location at Allen Boulevard and Menlo Drive in 1962. (Both, courtesy of Beaverton Christian Church.)

BETHEL CONGREGATIONAL
CHURCH, EARLY 1880s. In 1880,
three women met with Dr. George
Atkinson to discuss the possibility
of starting a Congregational
Church in Beaverton. Mrs. Klink
and the two Mrs. Andersons
must have been quite persuasive,
because within a year the Bethel
Congregational Church was
meeting regularly in the grange
hall at First and Stott Streets.
They purchased the building in
1881 and dedicated it as a chapel
in January 1882. In 1925, the
church relocated to property
on Watson Street purchased
from William Hocken. The
new church (below) featured a
community room with a stage
and kitchen as well as rooms for
a nursery and Sunday school
classes. (Both, courtesy of Bethel
Congregational Church.)

BETHEL CONGREGATIONAL CHURCH, 1925. Many hands make light work: moving the church piano to the new building on Watson Street required the assistance of several parishioners, including, from left to right, Mrs. George Stitt (still in the requisite black garb as she grieves her husband's 1924 death), Reverend Blanoliette, Dr. Harrison, and Reverend Ballinger. Fred Willis Cady, a very active member of the church, stands on the truck. Below, the interior of the church featured a gothic-style vaulted ceiling. (Both, courtesy of Bethel Congregational Church.)

Six

RECREATION AND CELEBRATIONS

Beaverton's residents have always made time for social gatherings and for celebrating together, and music was often a big part of the celebrations. The city bandstand provided a place for the Beaverton Band to put on open-air concerts for the public. On several occasions during the concerts, baskets of edible goods were auctioned off, with proceeds going directly to the band. The Beaverton Band also played at local events like boxing matches and was a regular addition to local parades.

Fourth of July celebrations usually included a parade down Broadway Street in which local businesses advertised on horse-drawn floats, the band marched, and children hoped to catch tossed candy. The city often participated in the Portland Rose Festival, decorating a flower-covered float to represent Beaverton. As for sports, baseball was a favorite pastime in Beaverton. The town boasted its own local team, which played against other local towns such as Banks, Forest Grove, Reedville, and Hillsboro.

Dances were regularly put on by different organizations around town, with lessons available as well. Walking to Morse Hall to attend a dance was a common and popular pastime in early Beaverton, as was going to the theater. At first, the Beaverton Grange was rented out to John Kamberger so that he could show the new form of entertainment to his fellow residents. He ran the projector and his wife played piano as accompaniment. In 1924, the city got its first actual theater, known alternately as the Beaver Theater and the Ritz Theater. It was a popular meeting place where one could watch a silent movie or take in a traveling show. When "talkies" were made available in 1929, interest in film increased and new theaters sprang up around town.

THE BEAVERTON BEAVERS, 1912. The Beaverton Beavers were at the top of their game during the 1912 and 1913 seasons. They were much admired by the community and supported by funds raised at local socials and dances. They won the championship in 1913 on a field just east of the Oregon Electric depot. The team included, from left to right, (first row) Mr. Behrman, F. Stroud, and Mr. Porth; (second row) H. Akin, Guy Alexander, O. Akin, Lev Hardy, Mr. Martin, L. Hughson, and Carl Desinger.

HOOK AND LADDER COMPANY, FOURTH OF JULY 1901. Beaverton's first hook and ladder company marches in the Fourth of July parade of 1901. Earl Fisher marches with his fife and bugle alongside drummer Earl Evans, as Walter Chatterton marches along with a cant hook tool and Harry Summers displays the company's ladder. It was not until 1919 that the city purchased a hose cart, 500 feet of hose, and a cart that could hold two 15-gallon tanks of water.

BEAVERTON BAND, 1910.
The Beaverton Military
Band entertained at many
events in and around
Beaverton and had a
standing gig at the town
bandstand on Broadway
Street where local
women would auction off
carefully prepared picnic
baskets, with the proceeds
supporting the band. They
played at many local events
at the Grange Hall and
the bandstand and were
regulars at the annual
Fourth of July parade.

PARADE FLOAT, C. 1912.
Vena Thyng, daughter
of confectioner George
Thyng, and Violet Sprainer
enjoy a ride on the parade
float in 1912. Beaverton's
Broadway Street was the
usual venue for the annual
Fourth of July parade and
Rose Parade festivities.
(Courtesy of Judy Donovan.)

FOURTH OF JULY PARADE, 1912. Beaverton's Fourth of July celebrations have always included a festive parade down Broadway Street. Floyd Allen had the honor of serving as grand marshal in 1912. In this photograph, horse-drawn floats pass by the Rossi Saloon and Thyng's Confectionery.

FOURTH OF JULY, 1912. Children gather at what is likely the banana split booth at the Fourth of July celebration. Lillian Thyng of Thyng's Confectionery offered her homemade toppings piled high on ice cream shipped from Portland on the special day. The sweet-tooths include, from left to right, (first row) Vallie Stitt, Violet Fleck, Harold Kelly, Vena Thyng, Lillian Thyng, Louie Hughson, George Thyng, Bob Summers, and Stanley Summers; (second row) Mathilda Kelley, Mrs. George Stitt, Horace Emmons, and Viola Shepards.

INDEPENDENCE DAY PARADE, C. 1920S. Parade watchers line Broadway Street to see the annual Fourth of July parade in the early 1920s. Rossi Saloon is on the left and Morse Hall, home of Thyng's Confectionery, is on the right. Local farmer John Frohnauer uses the opportunity to advertise his lettuce and cucumbers on his horse-drawn wagon.

PORTLAND ROSE FESTIVAL PARADE, 1926. The Portland Rose Festival and its Grand Floral Parade have been an annual tradition since 1907. Beaverton's entry in the 1926 parade was this flower-covered float praising Beaverton as a "city of homes" and all-around good place to raise a family. In this photograph, the elaborately decorated float rounds the corner of West and Broadway Streets, with the confectionery and White Hall visible in the background.

FORD CELEBRATION, 1931. Beaverton residents celebrate the 20-millionth Ford car in front of the Bank of Beaverton on Watson Street and Farmington Road. Albert Wilson, mayor of Beaverton several times during the 1930s, is at the wheel. Also shown are Doy Gray of the Bank of Beaverton (left of car with arms crossed) and local undertaker Winfield E. Pegg (left of man holding white hat). Although the country was in the throes of the Great Depression, many came out to celebrate the success of the Ford Motor Company, well known in Beaverton due to Otto Erickson's Ford business. A year later, in 1932, Ford introduced the V-8 engine and began producing mid-price cars like the Ford Mercury. Unfortunately for Beaverton, Otto Erickson closed his business by the mid-1930s.

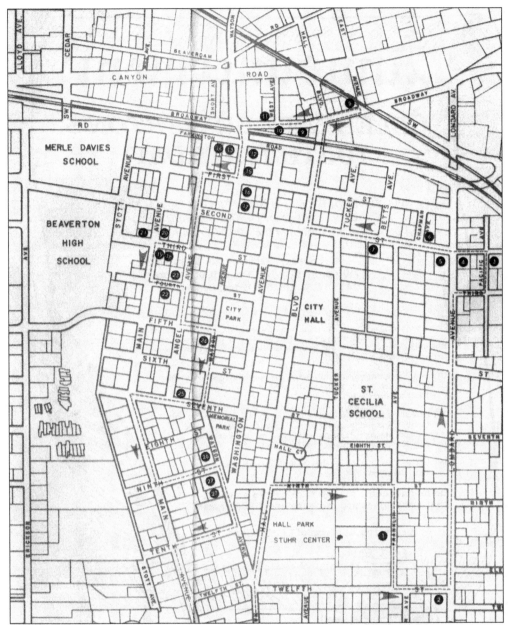

HISTORICAL TOUR MAP. Beaverton is proud of the many historical buildings still standing in and around the downtown core. This tour map highlights the commercial buildings of yesteryear as well as the homes of several early residents, such as Fred Willis Cady, the Hockens, the Desingers, Dr. Francis Robinson, and the Thyngs. (Courtesy of the Beaverton City Planning Department.)

BEAVERTON'S CENTENNIAL CELEBRATION, 1993. In celebration of the city's 100th birthday, a party was held in Griffith Park in early 1993. There were wagon rides, special postal cancellations for those who brought letters, and a press conference with the mayor. In the evening, a reception was held at city hall. Festivities continued around the city through November of that year, including a centennial fashion show, screenings of Premium Pictures films in May, and a pioneer reunion in October. (Courtesy of the City of Beaverton.)

BIBLIOGRAPHY

Beaverton Masonic Lodge No. 100. *Highlights: 100 Years.* Beaverton, OR: 1991.

Bethel Congregational Church. *The Bethel Story: Our First One Hundred Years.* Beaverton, OR: 1980.

Buan, Carolyn M. *This Far-off Sunset Land: A Pictorial History of Washington County, Oregon.* Virginia Beach, VA: The Donning Company Publishers, 1999.

———. "Land of the Beavers." *Historian,* Vol. 4. 2007.

Carr, Guy. *Guy Carr: A Memoir – the First Fifty Years.* Forest Grove, OR: Meridith L. Bliss, 1993.

Herrschaft, Winn. "Otto Erickson, A Man of Indomitable Spirit." *Historian,* Vol. 4. 2007.

———. "The Fanno Family." *Historian,* Vol. 4. 2007.

Mapes, Virginia. *Chakeipi: The Place of the Beaver.* Beaverton, OR: City of Beaverton, 1993.

Schoenberg, Wilfred P. *These Valiant Women: History of the Sisters of St. Mary of Oregon, 1886–1986.* Beaverton, OR: Sisters of St. Mary in Oregon, 1986.

Scott, Ken. "The Resistance." *Air & Space/Smithsonian.* Washington, DC: Smithsonian Enterprises, May 2007.

United States Department of the Interior. *National Park Service, National Register of Historic Places Inventory Nomination Form.* 1986.

Varner, Gerald. *School Days.* Beaverton, OR: Beaverton School District, 2000.

Visit us at
arcadiapublishing.com

CPSIA information can be obtained
at www.ICGtesting.com
Printed in the USA
LVOW04*1015130217

524101LV00015B/61/P